Butterflies

Victoria Blakemore

For Laura, my PLC buddy and friend

© 2018 Victoria Blakemore

vblakemore.author@gmail.com

Copyright info/picture credits

Table of Contents

What Are Butterflies?

Butterflies are a kind of insect. They are closely related to moths.

There are about 20,000 different species of butterflies. They have different coloring, wing shape, and live in different places.

Butterflies are usually more brightly colored than moths. They are also more likely to be seen during the day.

Size

Butterflies can be different sizes. The smallest kind of butterfly is the blue pygmy butterfly. It has a **wingspan** of about half an inch.

The largest is the Queen Alexandria birdwing. It has a **wingspan** of up to twelve inches.

Many butterflies are between

three and five inches from

wing tip to wing tip.

Physical Characteristics

Butterflies have two antennae on their head. Their antennae help them to smell. They can also help the butterfly to balance.

Like other insects, butterflies have three body parts: the head, **thorax**, and **abdomen**. They also have six legs.

Butterflies have tiny scales on their wings. The scales give butterfly wings their bright colors.

Habitat

Butterflies live in many habitats.

They live in forests, deserts,

mountains, grasslands, and

marshes.

Many butterflies **migrate** to

warmer places when it gets

cold. This is because they can't

fly if they are too cold.

Butterflies are found on every

continent except Antarctica.

There are over 2,000 species of butterflies found in North America.

Diet

Butterflies are **herbivores**.

They only eat parts of plants.

When they are still
caterpillars, they eat leaves
and flowers. When they are
fully grown, they drink nectar
from flowers and juice from
fruits.

Butterflies use a straw-like tube called a **proboscis** to drink nectar from flowers.

Butterflies are **attracted** to certain flowers. They are also **attracted** to sugar water.

Some people have a butterfly garden. They plant flowers that butterflies like. They also have special butterfly feeders. The feeders are filled with sugar water.

Communication

Butterflies use chemicals, sound, and movement to send messages to other butterflies. They have special chemicals that they can use to **attract** other butterflies.

Some butterflies make clicking sounds. They are used to defend their space.

Butterflies use movements like hard wing flapping to defend themselves or flowers they are feeding on.

17

Movement

Butterflies are able to fly at different speeds. The shape of their wings makes a big difference to how fast they can fly. Most fly between five and ten miles per hour.

Faster butterflies, such as skippers, can fly up to twenty-five miles per hour.

Butterflies cannot fly if they are

too cold or if their wings are

wet.

Butterflies lay their eggs on plants. Most lay their eggs on leaves, but there are some that lay their eggs on the stem.

Caterpillars hatch out of the eggs. When they first hatch, they eat the egg shell they came out of.

Caterpillars eat as many plants as they can. They need to eat a lot before they form their chrysalis or pupa.

Caterpillars spin a **cocoon** from silk. Their cocoon protects the chrysalis as it **transforms** into a butterfly.

When the butterfly is ready, it breaks open the **cocoon** and comes out. Later, when the butterfly lays eggs, it lays them on a plant the caterpillars that hatch can eat.

After their **metamorphosis**,

butterfly wings are wet. They

need to let them dry before

they can fly.

Self Defense

Butterflies have different ways to protect themselves from predators like birds, frogs, and other insects.

Some butterflies use cryptic coloring, which is when the color of their wings confuses predators.

One example of this is the owl
butterfly. It has spots on its
wings that look like an owl's
eyes.

Some butterflies are poisonous to animals. They can make animals very sick if they are eaten.

Poisonous butterflies are usually very brightly colored. Their bright colors warn predators that they are poisonous and should not be eaten.

The monarch butterfly is one

example of a poisonous

butterfly.

Population

Many butterfly populations are **declining**. Some butterflies, like the karner blue butterfly, are **endangered**. Some butterflies are already **extinct**.

Butterflies are facing threats such as habitat loss, **climate change**, and pollution.

In the wild, most butterflies live

for about a month. There are a

few kinds that live up to nine

months.

Helping Butterflies

There are many groups that are trying to help butterflies. One way that groups are helping is by counting and tracking butterflies.

Researchers need to know how many butterflies are in different places so they can help to protect them.

Special **preserves** are set up in many countries. They provide animals like butterflies with a safe habitat.

Many people help butterflies in their garden by planting flowers that butterflies like. Plants like milkweed and fennel provide butterflies with food and a place to lay eggs.

Glossary

Abdomen: the part of an insect's body that contains the heart and digestive organs

Attract: to cause something to come near

Attracted: made to come near, gained the attention of

Climate: the usual weather in a particular place

Cocoon: the hard outer covering that a caterpillar makes before becoming a butterfly

Declining: getting smaller

Endangered: at risk of becoming extinct

Extinct: when there are no more of an animal left in the wild

Herbivore: an animal that eats only plants

Metamorphosis: the changes a living thing goes through as it grows

Migrate: to move from one place to another

Preserves: areas of land set up to protect plants and animals

Proboscis: the straw-like tube a butterfly uses to drink nectar

Thorax: the middle part of an insect's body, where the wings attach to the body

Transforms: changes

Wingspan: the distance between the tips of an animal's wings

About the Author

Victoria Blakemore is a first grade

teacher in Southwest Florida with a

passion for reading.

You can visit her at

www.elementaryexplorers.com

Also in This Series

Gray Wolves	Sloths	Flamingos	Camels	Koalas	Honey Bees	Pandas
Pangolins	White-Tailed Deer	Orcas	Giraffes	Corn	Meerkats	Echidnas
Walruses	Raccoons	Bald Eagles	Apples	Arctic Foxes	Red Pandas	Cassowaries
Tigers	Ladybugs	Moose	Beluga Whales	Leopards	Elephants	Jellyfish
Binturongs	Lions	Dolphins	Reindeer	Hammerhead Sharks	Hippos	Pumpkins
Peafowl	Chameleons	Florida Panthers	Aye-Ayes	Black Bears	Cheetahs	Manatees
Gingerbread	Polar Bears	Hot Chocolate	Orangutans	Coyotes	Marshmallows	Strawberries

Elementary Explorers

Victoria Blakemore

Also in This Series

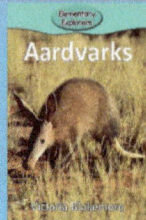

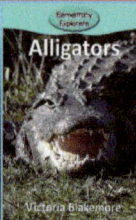

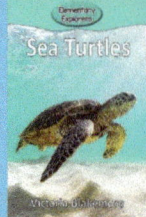

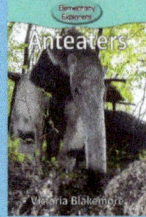

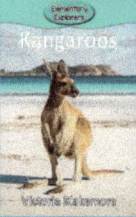

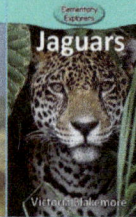

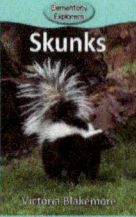

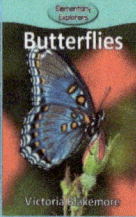

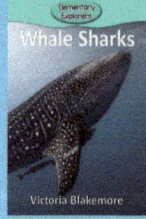

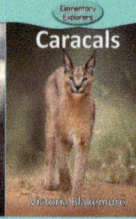

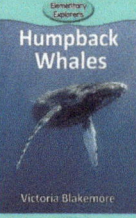

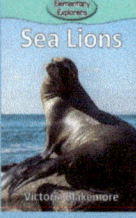

Aardvarks	Mako Sharks	Alligators	Frogs	Hedgehogs	Brown Bears	Bongos
Sea Turtles	Quokkas	Muskrats	Zebras	Red Foxes	Ring-Tailed Lemurs	Platypuses
Anteaters	Kangaroos	Rhinos	Jaguars	Wombats	Capybaras	Gorillas
Cats	Skunks	Butterflies	Dingoes	Snow Leopards	African Wild Dogs	Penguins
Whale Sharks	Wolverines	Warthogs	Caracals	Badgers	Seals	Hummingbird
Pikas	Humpback Whales	Pumas	Lemonade	Llamas	Tulips	Ostriches
Sunflowers	Fennec Foxes	Sea Lions	Squirrels	Roses	Porcupines	Ice Cream

All titles by Victoria Blakemore — Elementary Explorers

www.ingramcontent.com/pod-product-compliance
Lightning Source LLC
Chambersburg PA
CBHW051250020426
42333CB00025B/3151